# Ash 99

Daniel Luke Nunley

authorHOUSE®

AuthorHouse™
1663 Liberty Drive
Bloomington, IN 47403
www.authorhouse.com
Phone: 1-800-839-8640

Published by AuthorHouse 7/26/2012

ISBN: 978-1-4772-4034-2 (sc)
ISBN: 978-1-4772-4033-5 (e)

Library of Congress Control Number: 2012912430

for alison

*"Where did love begin? What human being looked at another and saw in their face the forests and the sea? Was there a day, exhausted and weary, dragging home food, arms cut and scarred, that you saw yellow flowers and, not knowing what you did, picked them because I love you?"*

Jeanette Winterson

For the first time in my life, I'm stumped. Utterly stumped. I have had writer's block before. Many times, actually. This is something fundamentally different.

I can write little comedy articles, blogs about my job, self-absorbed "tweets"...but I can't seem to create anything of merit, anything of value for what I consider my most important (and pressing) project. It is especially frustrating because of what it is I'm supposed to be writing about, the dear importance of my subject and the high esteem in which I hold it.

I consider myself a poor poet at most times. Oddly enough, it seems my best work is produced while I am semi-conscious. According to a few of those close enough to witness it, there are times when I spout out some improvised lines while I am asleep (often in the Old English tongue, I'm told.) Admittedly, there are times that I remember this. I have woken up before with fresh ideas and a renewed energy.

But there is something now that prevents me from cultivating any creative energy I might have and focusing it where I am supposed to. It constantly changes, it seems, and stirs about ceaselessly, as if it is searching for something. A reprieve, perhaps. Some relief. The answer to a question too provocative to truly, deeply contemplate.

It is uncertainty.

The idea was simple enough. It had been done thousands of times before, throughout much of recorded history. William Shakespeare, E.E. Cummings, the biblical King Solomon...one would be hard pressed to find any popular or influential writer (or any writer, for that matter) who has not written in dedication to a love. Man or woman, young or old, out of admiration or joy, anger or grief...the things we find to difficult to say out loud have often been said with pen and paper. So it seemed a simple enough task to write a few poems for you.

Except there is nothing simple about you.

You are truly something complex. You are a deeply intricate and diverse creature, a person very much different than any I've met before or expect to meet in the future. It is normally very easy for me to deconstruct someone, peeling away the layers, the masks, the inhibitions, all the subtleties to discover the true nature hiding away inside. (It's what makes me an effective salesman, and a completely awkward party guest.)

There is a certain danger in this sort of scrutinizing. I've only begun to really discover that this is not a socially acceptable thing to do, at least not if it is done in a way that is readily apparent anyway. It can be misconstrued as arrogance, and I am starting to understand and appreciate the beauty of approaching someone without bias or prejudice, without passing judgment. It's a beautiful thing to be surprised, and equally as beautiful and painful to be fooled.

But you? I can't figure out. At all. I've never been able to pin you down one way or another. You're my great contradiction.

Perhaps it is inappropriate, wholly unfair to you, for me to try. (Although it is a subconscious occurrence more often than not, the fact that I am readily aware of it means I ultimately have control.)

The discovery, for me, is fun, and rewarding. The more layers it seems I peel away, the more I discover, and the deeper your mystery becomes.

Maybe that's why I am so attracted to you. You are a mystery.

I have absolutely lost myself in you. You've wrapped me up so tightly, so sweetly that I couldn't ever escape, even if I wanted to. It's terrifying.

There is a certain unspoken ( or unacknowledged) truth in relationships that is fundamentally simple and wholly unavoidable, in that the more time you spend with someone, the more like the other you become. Some people seem to be afraid of this, seeing it as a theft of their personal identity, which I believe is a shallow or perhaps apprehensive interpretation of what is happening. I haven't so much lost my identity as I have given it over to yours. You are the other side of the equation. I find my dreams, my happiness, and my life in the brightness and hope that you give to me.

To use a classical cliché, you are the missing piece of the puzzle. The better half of who I am, and who I want to be.

But you are so, so much more.

I cannot give you words to describe my adoration. I cannot express in words the gratitude in my heart for the gift that you are to me, as a friend, a guide, a partner. That you would choose to share your time with me is astounding. That you'd give me the honor of sharing your life is beyond comprehension.

I hope I can live up to it someday.

"Words cannot describe my love for you." It is a cliché, I understand. But it is one that truly applies.

Unfortunately, all I can offer to you are my words, and the promise that I will try to live up to them, and to the mystery of who you are.

And my love. You have all of that, and more.

"It is by no means an irrational fancy that, in a future existence, we shall look upon what we think of our present existence, as a dream."

Edgar Allan Poe

how do you tell someone you love them?
do you say it every day
and look in their eyes so they
know you're sincere?
do you shout it to the world
empty your lungs to let everyone
know you've been taken?
do you whisper it in their ear
softly, sweetly, so you
know they have heard?
do you put it in a song
and sing it from your heart to
know the truth of the chorus?
do you write it in a book
and immortalize your words, so they
know it is eternal?
how do you tell someone you love them?
you can't
no matter how hard you try
to tell someone you love them
it is only words that you offer
you may mean it
but they will never
know it for sure
for your love to know
you cannot tell them
with only words
for your love to know you love them
you must show it
how do you tell someone you love them?
you show them

*"It is not true that love makes things easy: it makes us choose what is difficult."*

*George Eliot*

it is so deafeningly silent
the dryer, with its rattling and whining
with every spin and cycle and rotation
growing louder, louder
more painful, more maddening
the traffic on the road
whirring tires and steaming, roaring engines
every inconsiderate person pushing
more and more forcefully on
their stressed throttles as
they rocket past my open door that
shakes and rattles and screams
motorbikes and passenger cars and
every large truck it seems sets their route
to fly through the street in front of my home in
the most obtrusive of ways, ever vengeful and
distracting and an annoyance
so i sit in front of the television, set the volume
as high as it can go, and desperately
attempt to drown out the irritating noises
thinking and screaming to the sound
of the same movies played over and
over again over all these months
and this of course all adds up to somehow, inexorably
to that deafening silence
where every single sound that
pushes its way into my ears
only reminds me of the silence
between us
days and weeks and months with only

10

as much as a few words and change here and there
and as little as indifference
but only in the silence, that creeping
mystery and terror and fog
have i really heard your voice
its nature, its desires
its truth
i may have forgotten its sound
its pitch, its timbre
i may have forgotten your inflections
how you enunciate, the way you speak my name
how you say that four letter word and
how sweetly it used to cross my ears
i may have forgotten your voice
but i hear it now
it resonates deeply within the
shattered pits and valleys of uncertainty
and echoes, bounces, clangs around in the
canyon of my head
reverberating
with the intensity of a tangible eternity
only in the silence have i heard your voice
screaming loudly now
over the traffic outside my door
over the selfish cries of iniquity
and my languid indifference
i close my door and listen
through the noise
you are there
in the silence
you are there

"One of the remarkable things about love is that, despite very irritating people writing poems and songs about how pleasant it is, it really is quite pleasant."

Daniel Handler (as Lemony Snicket)

The problem with most "love" poetry is the tendency to abandon what could be reasonably, believably true in favor of the flowery metaphor or the scintillating line describing the subject's divine beauty or perfection. The poet often makes a deity of the subject.

The flaw of poetry as presentation is often an insistence on the untrue. In the case of poetry written for a love interest, this manifests itself as a makeover of the subject. Whether wholly complex and utterly simple in its execution, the target of a hormone-induced "love and desire" tirade constructed as poetry is always made to seem a perfect being without flaw or vice.

But people are never perfect.

Take me, for example. I'm quite flawed, in numerous ways, some mundane, others much too embarrassing to put into print.

For example...

1.  I have an eye for the fantastic or impractical, and so often I can lose myself in a pursuit which many would deem a waste of time or energy.
2.  I eat too much and too often, while I complain ever concurrently about what miserable shape my body is in.
3.  I tend to lose interest in a task rather quickly, which is a terrible quality for those of us (read, everyone) who need to work for a living.
4.  I'm something of a nerd, although it wouldn't be so noticeable to a stranger. I hide it well...sometimes.
5.  I snore, loudly.
6.  I burn easily in the sun, so I'm often no fun at the beach. (Aside from the copious amounts of sunscreen I must wear, which I'm told is a rather humorous sight.)
7.  Speaking of which, I have an irrational fear of sharks, which extends itself not only to swimming in the ocean but even to a backyard pool thousands of miles away. You never know...there could be sharks in there...
8.  I'm kind of a hairy guy. I have my father to thank for that. It's not something

uncommon, but I find it quite annoying. There is a particular spot on my left shoulder that keeps sprouting a single black hair, and one day I am sure it will drive me into a blind rage in the grooming aisle of a local supermarket.

9. I tend to be a bit vain when it comes to my appearance, if you couldn't tell.

10. I sweat easily. Not an amount that would make you want to recoil, but enough to justify why I'm constantly drinking water (and therefore constantly thirsty.) It's more of a personal annoyance, if anything, but it bears mentioning.

The beauty of being able to say these things, no matter how inappropriate or embarassing, is the fact that they make me normal. There are people all over the world who could be described similarly and yet still be quite different. It is not a bad thing to be normal when you consider how inescapable a quality it is.

To be perfect; that would be weird.

As easy as it is for me to roll off some of these weird things about me, it's just as difficult for me to name any of yours.

This is not to say you are perfect; that is not my intention, understand. It does say something though that I can't quite think of a trait in you to exploit or explore, which is the job of an honest writer. In that regard I consider myself a failure.

You know, I find myself attracted to who you are in every way despite the ways in which I feel I fail you.

Sometimes I know we aren't communicating the way we should. I blame myself as much as anything. It takes an unprecedented level of trust and comfort to open yourself up to someone, especially in such an intimate way. It is a trust I hope to build.

Regardless of that, I find myself enthralled in you and your life, your family, your dreams, your prayers. So it would be unfair of me to reduce who you are and what you mean to me into a metaphor, since no amount of imagery or adverbs can carry with them the feelings and motivations which would justify being written. This is the challenge of a poet: the pitfalls of such purple prose would be to seem a half-hearted, half thought out, and half finished effort at best. You deserve truth, and maybe a laugh or two.

Or ten. Maybe ten laughs would be nice.

it's in the way she moves and the way she speaks

the way she flips her hair

the way her hand feels in mine and the

softness of her skin

the way her head falls on my shoulder

and the simplest things i take for granted

she breathes new life into them

the way she sits and the way she stands

and every step she takes

the way she speaks and her quick smile

the way she laughs

especially her laugh

it's the shape of her hips and

her nose and her lips

and the way her eyes sparkle

when i look into them

her dreams are big, her

heart is bigger

and she whispers softly to me

those words that give me flight

but it is not in her words or even the

meaning behind them that i find joy

its in the way she says them

in the way she shows them

in the way she is

and how she makes me

who i want to be

the way she is

the way i am with you

the way we are

is where i find my joy

"If a man can be properly said to love something, it must be clear that he feels affection for it as a whole, and does not love part of it to the exclusion of the rest."

Plato

i bring you your yellow rose and some little cards
i write out a line or two that i think will make you smile
and i hope to earn your love
i bring you your yellow rose and make a little joke
and i tickle you a little, softly
and i hope to earn your laughter
i bring you your yellow rose and i put in on your car
because work was hard and this might help
and i hope to earn your gratitude
i bring you your yellow rose and hold out my arms
for a hug, and plant a kiss on your cheek
and i hope to earn your affection
i bring you your yellow rose because
it makes you smile
and i hope to earn every one
and yet i feel unworthy of your smile
your laughter, gratitude
your affection
your love
i bring you your yellow rose
and i hope to earn you

but you, like that rose you hold in your hand

or the one that lays on your car

or the one i leave at your door

you are a gift

and a gift is not something to be earned

so let me say i'm sorry for

trying to earn your laughter with

every corny joke

let me say i'm sorry for

my silly attempts to

make you smile

let me say i'm sorry for

maybe being closed to your

true affection

and let me say i'm sorry for

not showing you

my gratitude

your love is a gift that i could

never deserve

i bring you your yellow rose

as a gift in return

i bring you your yellow rose because i love you

*"Why does a man who is truly in love insist that this relationship must continue and be "lifelong"? Because life is pain and the enjoyment of love is an anesthetic. Who would want to wake up halfway through an operation?"*

Cesare Pavese

I could maybe write a dirty limerick or something to get a cheap laugh out of you, but that doesn't seem fair. After all, my whole flirting game is based on those cheap laughs. Using them all up in a little poem would just completely ruin the spontaneous nature of my flirting, and then what reason do you have to spend time with me? Other than to see my pretty face. (You can't fool me; I know you've been looking.)

Oh, by the way, I understand you're afraid of roller coasters. What's the big deal, you weenie? They just strap you in to a little rickety cart with a thin seatbelt (or sometimes no restraints at all, just a little orange thing to hold on to) and then send you flying high into the air at exceptionally dangerous speeds that would easily kill you if something were to go wrong.

But what could possibly go wrong on a highly complicated, industrially structured machine that is repeatedly used for years on end? I mean, it was built with the sole intention of putting you into a potentially dangerous situation that could kill you in moments at the slightest malfunction.

What's there to possibly be afraid of?

(Let it be known that the author is, in fact, being facetious and is well aware of the safety and maintenance procedures of our world's finest amusement ride construction and engineering firms. Let it also be known that the author is, himself, deathly terrified of roller coasters but still enjoys them on a consistent basis. Also, the tilt-a-whirl is a madman's death wish. ALSO also, the author is not genuinely making fun of or critiquing the subject of this discourse in any way, and is only seeking a slight chuckle from the reader, one which he will surely pay for at such a time when it is read. I love you, honey, so please put down the golf club.)

We share a mutual fear of sharks in ridiculous situations. What is wrong with us? I really think we should seek some kind of fear counseling, maybe even visit an aquarium with a shark exhibit. We can work our way up to diving with sharks. Won't that be fun?

(Let it be known that at the time of this writing, the subject of this book, being the author's best friend and all around love of his life, is soon spending a week at the beach. While the author is indeed jealous of her relaxing adventures and wishes to do the same, the idea of jumping into an ocean full of sharks has now permeated his consciousness, and he now only sees this trip as an opportunity for some shark to eat his woman. Caveman instincts overtaking, "Ugg kill shark." Terrified. Hiring Quint.)

I really love spending time with you. I always want to be with you! But sometimes, for some reason, my nerves get the better of me and I sit there shaking uncontrollably.

And you laugh at me.

Not cool, babe. Not cool.

(Let it be known that the author believes it is, in fact, "cool", and that the subject of each previous remark is in his mind the "coolest". Yes, you.)

"Love…must come suddenly, with great thunderclaps and bolts of lightning-
a hurricane from heaven that drops down on your life, overturns it, tears away
your will like a leaf, and carries your whole heart off with it into the abyss."

Gustave Flaubert

at the most bitter edge

time and space and all

that lies in between

from the frayed edges of the galaxy to

the brightest stars in the sky

the depth and heart and truth of it all

is only this

that my heart so often finds its

way into my throat, time and time again

because I sit unaware of the thoughts that race through your head

the truest emotions that course through you

the pulse and vibration and all of

your life and intricacies

i have lost it

in time, like a river flowing ceaselessly, tirelessly, without fail

into nothing, falling into nothing

but still every fiber and strand of what i am

is marked with you, like a stain

(you may find this peculiar)

this is the ear within me

that listens for a ringing bell and

walks and chirps like a pesky bug

the terrible parasite that licks the detritus

of my stability, the erosion of every

function, perception, emotion

my structure

each time my heart leaps, each hour

that passes again and again and again

without remorse or effort or care

another piece of me falls away

i lay at that edge, crumbling, disintegrating

slowly (but horribly) eaten from the inside

yet you stand, looking me over like merchandise

and so seamless, so absent of affliction or scars

or any strand resembling me

soaring high, high

swiftly, weightlessly

to such great and terrible heights

past the edge of time

and the frayed tendrils of my galaxies

you become the sky that I find so painfully

tragically

out of reach

you remain my sky

you have infected me

this joyous, heavenly disease that you are

terminal

inoperable, aggressive, destructive

(in the most startling, beautiful, amazing of ways)

and the edges of existence crumble and

drop into the earth

swiftly, weightlessly

to such great and terrible depths

and you (my sky) engulf it all

on the edge

my heart clings to the remains of your presence

i have forgotten your scent

the sound of your laughter

the touch of your skin

but I cannot forget your essence

or the gift of your stain

you (my sky) remind me

of everything

*"If you live to be a hundred, I want to live to be a hundred minus one day so I never have to live without you."*

A .A. Milne

it was like electricity

The first time your hand grasped mine

and our fingers slipped past and through one another

Locked in some sort of symbolic predestinate bridge,

some indication of the trembling energy surging its
way from our hearts, souls, and stomachs

one to another like a

cosmic wave radiating fiercely, profoundly

building up and bubbling and growing more intense with
each second that passed and yet remained

somehow

calm, restrained

It almost felt dangerous

And as my head fell, finally, gratefully, sweetly into your lap

And your fingers searched their way across my chest,
tip toeing so delicately up my chin

skimming ever so briefly across the surface of my lips

I felt the weight of all the years of all existence lift from my broken
shoulders, and the universe came to such a sudden, violent halt

As if at that moment time and space and gravity froze

and nothing reverberated or hummed or made a noise
     but the pulse from your heart and mine

Slowly, strongly working their way into rhythm with one another

their energy fusing ceaselessly, colliding and crash-
     ing and becoming singular and unified

your heart and mine

Slowly, strongly working their way into rhythm with one another

Like some predetermined fate from long ago

A kiss on the wrist

And the universe began to breathe again

The room began to spin

And the truth, the undeniable fact had revealed it-
     self with such sudden ferocity

The universe had aligned

And that which was destiny had begun its journey in
     the most powerful but delicate of ways

The touch of your skin was an electric shock

The weight of your hand made the universe stand still

Your wrist on my lips sealed my fate

You became time and space

and I began to breathe

"It is difficult to know at what moment love begins; it
is less difficult to know that it has begun."

Henry Wadsworth Longfellow

Why did you think I shook so violently as we lay there
    (finally) pushed against one another

Holding on so tightly, it seems clutching that
    gift of time that had so eluded us

And you laughed so sweetly as every little pressure, ev-
    ery slight adjustment, every time our skin touched

I shook uncontrollably

and you kissed me again

this is what I miss most of all, I think

the way you move me

the way you can unmask all of my deepest wonderings

That way you can look at me for a brief mo-
    ment and cause the earth to shatter

You terrify me in the most beautiful of ways

And I believe, I know, I feel this is why I shake

Every laugh, every touch, every kiss

Peels away a layer of myself that isn't imbued with who you are

And replaces it fully with your every joy and despair, your de-
    sires, your heart, your darkness and your light

that shimmering blinding light

The remarkable and beautiful thing is that you, with all
    your grace and life and all of your subtleties

would choose to build your life and everything you are with me

this man who you can shake with nothing more than a
    look in the eye or a brief smile or a little laugh

I shake because you're breaking me

I shake because I'm losing myself to you

In the most reckless beautiful remarkable unex-
    plainable and joyous way possible

Even when you are gone I shake

And peel away another layer of myself

So I can replace it with you

with you

"Love does not begin and end the way we seem to think it does.
Love is a battle, love is a war; love is a growing up."

James A. Baldwin

fifty-six days

I've seen you all of two minutes in the past fifty-six days

but two minutes is all it takes

you'll never have any idea how violently my heart
        pounded as I was pulling away

sitting at that red light, I tried not to turn my head towards your car

where you sat, blissfully, so luminous and lovely

not more than fifty yards away

it just felt like a million miles

sitting at that red light, I began to shake

and all my breath was taken from me

if I write to you, if I sing you a song, if I send you my love

does the same wintry glance find its way back to me?

is your distance yet again multiplied?

do I continue to miss the way you used to light up when our eyes met

my beautiful golden fiery sun

will the warmth that left you fifty-six days ago flee far-
        ther and farther from my grasp?

will your presence continue to haunt me, and
        your absence deconstruct me?

sitting at that red light, your voice echoing in me
        even in all of your indifference

I feel a tug at my side, as if to tell me to return

to remind you

to write to you, to sing you a song

to give you my love

fifty-six days, two minutes, and one red light later

I turn away and breathe

I will write to you

sing you a thousand songs

give you all of my love

I will return to you

and we will be reminded

*"Love is being stupid together."*
Paul Valery

if I continue on with this aimlessness, this lack of direction, this facade of contentedness...if I choose to live without passion, without intensity, without pride... without a destination...if I resign myself to the implacable vessel, pursuing ever forward the vastness of nothing, if I pursue that which is without trace or signature, if I do not throw myself overboard and sweetly, without struggle or remorse, sink into the hollow place beneath the waves...if I continue to draw breath and exhale death in its ashy shadowy smoke...if by some otherworldly means I am burned in the molecular fire...if I flee to the absent shelter and melt in the rain, the acid, the slow toxic envelopment of the clouds...if I bleed what remains of my existence into the fabric of space, the deep dark void...if I give up...if I live without you...time itself will stop (again)

and the universe will shatter

*"Love is an act of endless forgiveness, a tender look which becomes a habit."*

*Peter Ustinov*

this dampness is lonely
we worry behind our mouths
about the depths of true affection
and what could we ever know
is true other than our faith
it takes a great leap
a step towards the blazing fire that
can burn so easily but may yet
lovingly warm instead
alight on the winding path
that snakes away into uncertainty
but we take that journey
hand in hand
it is work and time
that in the end becomes something
joyful and beautiful
behind our lips lie questions
too provocative to ask yet
too significant to ignore
the truth may make itself difficult
to swallow but we are there
together
you and i

the past may haunt one
or the other along the journey
blameless though we be the
past always troubles our hearts
but the memories we wish to forget
are always subdued by grace
we will not be compared to those
ghosts of the past
those lingering specters that
imbue every hovering wish
with doubt
only through trust can we
tear apart that doubt
and leave our loneliness in ruin
with patience, kindness
and compassion and understanding
and self-control and especially
love
we become one, inexplicably
wonderfully, frighteningly linked
for a lifetime
and in that lifetime of forever
we discover that which defies
the very nature of comprehension
the nature of love

*"I was about half in love with her by the time we sat down. That's the thing about girls. Every time they do something pretty…you fall half in love with them, and then you never know where the hell you are."*

J. D. Salinger

The thing that no one will ever tell you about love is that it's so incredibly awkward. It's like every day is your high school prom, or a big job interview, or a first date. (It's A LOT like a first date.)

If you make a date with your significant other, it really doesn't matter what you'll be doing, or how much time you expect to spend with them: you will be taking an obsessive sort of shower.

You're going to be making sure you don't leave any patch of skin untouched. You're going to be using your special "date" soap that has the particular scent they always compliment. You'll be sure to use conditioner just in case they decide to play with your hair. Chances are you're going to shave.

You'll be using the "good" toothpaste. You'll floss and be sure to use your mouthwash for the full 30 seconds (or 60, depending on your level of commitment.)

Of course you'll have to break out the special perfume or cologne that they just love. (It's a mad dash to the store when you realize you're out of it.)

What's that? You're going to go see a movie and have a cheeseburger? Better wear your designer jeans and your nicest pair of shoes.

It's completely normal to want to look and feel your best around your partner. You can't slip up on a date! Which makes it all the funnier (and more frustrating) when disaster strikes.

You dropped the popcorn trying to sit down. Maybe you get some sort of sauce on your clothes. You knocked over your beverage in that nice restaurant. (And it's always a full glass.)

The coup de grâce has got to be when your credit card gets declined.

The thing that most people tend to forget is that for all the silly things that you do to prepare or every embarrassing thing you do in front of your partner, they've done the exact same thing. It's a beautiful, funny sort of thing that we always try to put our best foot forward for them (which does go a way to show we care enough about them to go through all that) but in the end we love not for our perfections but for our flaws.

For being able to laugh when you spill a drink. For the funny way they snort when they laugh. For watching those barriers fall down.

We are our true selves when this happens.

I am glad that I am able to be my totally obnoxious, awkward self around you. I'm thankful for that. It's a blessing that when I'm with you I can completely drop my guard and just let things be. I'm happiest when I'm with you.

I consider it a good sign when you can wear sweatpants and an old t-shirt, and I find you just as cute as you are in your best outfit. I'd take a quiet night at home with you over a night out any day.

Besides, if we stay in on a date, there's less chance I have of spilling coke all over the table.

*"Love is when you meet someone who tells you something new about yourself."*

*Andre Breton*

pineapple dreams and
banana sunsets
wild world of ticklish
pumpkin seeds and
dancing kiwis
strawberry delights the
pear is unusually popular
its american pie
orange tornados and
lemon hurricanes
the rain is lime
it's the parade of the century
the grand marshal mr. honeydew
is tossing grapes to the crowd
there is a raffle for
a great big cantaloupe
star fruit can-can and
peach motorcades
the apricots are jealous
the lesser fruits!
navels and tangerines
oh, and the tangelos
tag along, invisible
the grapefruit savior
with its ruby red
sweetness it's the
only hope for the
strange man
oh, the lesser fruits!
so insignificant their
plea so tinny their voices
perhaps only the god apple
can determine their fate

"The hours I spend with you I look upon as sort of a perfumed garden, a dim twi-
light, and a fountain singing to it. You and you alone make me feel that I am alive.
Other men it is said have seen angels, but I have seen thee and thou art enough."

George Edward Moore

if i could write of your beauty in a way that was worthy

if i could describe the anxiousness and sharpness and
      the yearning i feel when you look at me

if i could discover the words that would be perfect to you
      like a treasure that was golden and lustrous

if my thoughts and desires could carry weight and become tangible

if you could peer into me and who i am and what i find in you

if we could know each other's affections in and out

if i could absorb some sort of assurance from your skin

if i could deserve you for who you are and who you make me

if i could tell you of how you are time and stars and the moon and sun

if i could describe my love in words of how you are the ho-
      rizon and the fore and everything in between

if you could truly know the shape and breadth of my heart for yours

if the words i said could resemble at all the source

if you could uncover the depth and significance of who you are

if i could somehow erase the worst of my forgeries

if you could know that you are everything

if i could write of your beauty in a way that was worthy

you would know the deepest truths

and i may someday be worthy

*"Affection is responsible for nine-tenths of whatever solid and durable happiness there is in our lives."*

*C. S. Lewis*

There has been much written on the emotions of women, and the differences in how women interpret things versus how men interpret them.

I think we understand men fairly well; women will always be the big mystery. It IS certain, however, that women tend to be very fickle, perhaps especially in relationships.

Men tend to be thought of as aloof, or singularly motivated by sex. Women, on the other hand, seem to be thought of as the ultimate in sincerity.

This may often be true, especially in the formative years. But as the social liberation of women climaxed, things changed radically.

In the greater part of the western world, the female has become as socially integrated and emotionally, spiritually, and sexually free as men always were. Young girls are no longer betrothed at such early ages; they choose who they will marry. They are not looked down upon for their career choices or their financial standing (although such stigmas still exist, they are generally perceived as ignorant or narrow-minded.)

Are women judged harsher than men when it pertains to their lifestyle choices? Yes, but that gap is closing faster and faster.

This is all how it should be. Women and men are equal, and should always be treated as such.

Except, women and men aren't really all that equal…women have always been the more powerful of the species.

Women give us the gift of life. The day a man can carry and deliver a baby is the day the sexes will be equal…maybe.

Believe what you will, but most of recorded and significant history can be attributed to a man's desire for a woman, or to prove himself as worthy (again, to women).

I don't honestly believe women understand men in love. Here's the thing, ladies: when a man has fallen in love with you, that's it. You're everything to him. You've hooked him for good, no matter what.

It is because of this that men tend to get insecure.

That "clinginess" is insecurity. That word has begun to carry some very negative connotations, and it really shouldn't. We all want to be reassured, especially in a relationship. It does us no good to put ourselves out there without such effort being reciprocated.

Let's say a man and a woman meet. This guy looks good, he's saying all the right things, and pulling all the right moves. He's got this girl falling head over heels for him. He tells her he loves her. She knows he's the one.

Then she sleeps with him and everything changes.

He's no longer charming, or gentle, or giving. He turns selfish, maybe aggressive in a way. It becomes obvious what this guy is all about.

It's a story that happens far too often. Sadly, girls will keep running back to those guys hoping to be gratified again, or maybe because they think he can change for them, or be "fixed".

But men hardly ever change.

Let's flip the script.

A man and a woman meet. They're having fun, enjoying each other's company. An attraction is almost immediate. Things develop, sometimes quickly, sometimes over time. They begin seeing each other more and more often, and they start to become intimate. Eventually the big "L" word is dropped. Everything seems to be perfect.

This guy is madly in love with this girl. She becomes his whole world; he finds his happiness in her alone. He wants to talk every second of every day. He gets upset if she doesn't make time for him every single day.

He's clingy, jealous, and possessive.

She can't live like that, as she shouldn't. She breaks up with him (even though she really doesn't want to. She'd rather work things out, but again, men hardly ever change). Obviously, he doesn't take this well.

Maybe it's rage, maybe its depression, maybe some horrible combination of the two. In any case, his response is almost never positive, and further deteriorates the relationship. It's beyond repair.

A healthy mind realizes that life will go on, and somewhere down the road, there will be a new relationship, and you may be ready then. But many times the mind of a heartbroken person is absolutely far from healthy. Break-ups are a leading cause of suicide.

Perhaps these are extremes, but a lesson can be learned from them.

Men are inherently insecure in relationships. Men know that women are ALWAYS being hit on by other guys. It's something that is laughed off in a confident, secure relationship. But if a man isn't being reassured of his partner's affection on an almost daily basis, it is natural for the mind to consider the things that we are so afraid of.

Is she seeing someone else? Is she tired of me? Does she just not love me anymore?

Men in love have a tendency to become predictable, which can be dangerous in a young relationship (or any relationship for that matter). Women can become bored with predictable, and sometimes it may feel like the spark or the desire has been taken out of the relationship.

On the same token, men need to feel desired in order for any relationship to work.

Clinginess and possessiveness are never desirable. But a little bit of jealousy in a relationship is healthy on both sides.

If we're texting you flirtatious messages, we're trying to keep the playfulness in our relationship alive. If we're just calling to say we love you, appreciate it. We mean it and want you to know it.

While we're on the subject, the widespread adoption of the text message has had a profound effect on relationships.

People are getting to know each other more and more over text at first. It's very beneficial, in that way. But it's created a serious disconnect in the way our relationships work versus how they probably should.

It's easy to misunderstand someone over a text message considering you can't take a person's tone into account. Is it convenient to text instead of call? Absolutely, but that convenience comes at the price of connection.

Text messages are very impersonal. That's unavoidable. Something like a phone call, on the other hand, is much more transparent. It's easy to hide yourself in a text message; not so much on the phone.

If we are calling, it's because we want to talk to you personally, not the surrogate you use for your messages. Sometimes, we really just want to hear your voice.

There is nothing wrong with text messaging. It's convenient, fun, and useful. It can be a great way to have conversations, about anything. But it's the ultimate shield against connection.

Ever been broken up with over a phone call?

How about over a text?

Which was more painful?

Guys, I can't stress this enough. If a girl asks you to text her instead of calling, do it. She doesn't need to give you a reason; just trust her, and if you're concerned about it for whatever reason, you can talk about it face to face. When you make an effort to understand each other instead of letting your insecurities dominate, you'll find a relationship infinitely more rewarding and secure than you thought you could know.

As for the jealousy, keep it to a healthy level guys. Give each other time to yourselves. Guys, go out with the boys. Girls, take a night with the ladies. Don't let your relationship saturate.

And for the love of everything you hold dear, be spontaneous. Surprise each other. Thank each other.

Show your love every day.

Enough of the disjointed rambling.

Maybe more poetry. Maybe.

*"There is nothing I could say that will make you love me. But there is nothing you could say that would make me not love you."*

*Daniel Luke Nunley*

if i could ever again find a love as sure as this
    the earth would cease to spin

and the stars would gaze upon us

when i touch the sizzling sun of your skin and the im-
    palpable rush of you washes over me i cease my
    pursuit of what i thought paramount

and discover that you are the destination

every time your eyes find mine they seem to so quickly avert

and the earth ceases to spin

and whenever you seem to recoil from my touch
    the ultraviolet wave crashes over me

and i burn up in the stars

if it were ever possible to express the bliss and agony you seem
    to stir in my substance we would never again doubt

and we could escape the spindly arms of the galaxy

can you feel the gravity you suck out of the room?

do you steal the breath you force from me?

does it hurt your skin when we burn?

if i could ever describe my love to you as it is, sure-
    ly and ceaselessly and without doubt

i could touch your skin and steal your breath
    and we could escape gravity

you are paramount

and the stars will gaze upon us

"At a glimpse, a grain of sand, I'm chained to the Great Room Chamber's floor of Your heart; Lo, the freedom in this residence…"

Sean McCarty

The car screeched to a stop, the whining brakes scraping metal to metal. He had been meaning to get them changed.

He peered over the dashboard towards her as he pulled roughly on the ignition key (it had been sticking lately) but she made no sign or gesture. She stared blankly over the tree line, illuminated by the red sunset, and seemed resigned to nothing but a warm ambiguity.

He knew.

There had been something going on for a while now, but he couldn't recall when it had begun. He only remembered the growing despondency, the broadening distance, the frequent stretches of silence…his patience had run out.

But it wasn't anger or confusion or hopelessness that he carried with him; it was fear. Fear of an unintended consequence, or a foregone conclusion. Fear of the absolute and the inevitable.

He knew.

He pushed open the car door and swung his feet out to the ground, not yet touching his feet to the pavement below him, not yet taking the first step towards the inescapable fact. Reaching into the backseat, he pulled the article from its clear, wet bag, delicately, carefully unfurling it to be as presentable as possible.

He wondered for a moment if he should even bother.

With his offering in hand, his feet hit the pavement. He walked, ever deliberately, toward her, the burning beams of the sunset peeking through the tree leaves and blinding him. She did not move as he approached. She stood motionless, staring out over the horizon as if she were searching for something.

Perhaps a word of truth or a merciful lie. Perhaps the right line and the right pitch and the right inflection.

As he grew closer to her, he could only reflect of the beauty he saw in her at this moment, as the lights bounced off of her into the atmosphere. Her shape and her strands were never more apparent, and the flood of regret rushed into him ever more mournfully, forcefully.

When he was upon her, he said nothing. She repeated. It could have been minutes, or hours, or that eternity that lies just beyond the edge of the tangible.

In the end, the silence remained.

He turned his body toward her side, and lifted his gift to her, raising it to her chest as she continued to look intently into the vast open air before her.

For a long moment, she did not move. His eyes fell to his feet. The finality of it had rung within him like a bell. He was abandoned.

He knew.

And then he felt her skin touch his.

He looked up, towards the gift, the yellow rose, extended in his right hand, her left wrapped around it. She had turned towards him. She was no longer immersed in the sky. She had come back to the earth, to the dirt and pavement, and the trees surrounding them in the waning sunlight.

Her eyes fixed intently upon his, staring into them like they were the red, fiery sun.

He stared back, astounded, and felt her hand slowly grace his cheek. In her eyes, the sun and the trees and the yellow rose reflected brilliantly, and glinted and winked at him.

He raised his hand to her face.

They let the rose fall to the ground.

In the setting sun they stood transfixed upon each other, wrapped up in the silence and the end and the beginning.

He knew.

They knew.

She only swayed a little when she was making dinner, her feet sore from the shoes she was forced to wear at work. She didn't resent her task or her tired feet, but the weariness she tried to hide was too deep to cover.

He in his spot on the couch, faded green and worn from years of use, sat as quietly as he could, only moving now and then to twist the cap from his bottle of soda.

"Do you want something to drink?" he offered her.

"No, thank you." was always her reply.

Always.

He couldn't help but watch a little at the subtle ways she shifted her position, resting on one foot and then the other. She was favoring her right foot tonight, he thought. She must have been doing payroll tonight, or something similar. The office work.

He had meant to bring her a milkshake at work that night. It slipped his mind. The tinge of guilt danced a bit in his stomach. He could see her shoulders sagging, her head hanging a little low, scrunched over the skillet where she softly plodded at the dinner she had said she'd make.

"I should be helping" he thought. "She's so tired."

It was red beans and rice that night, a simple meal. They had made it before, and her particular way was a mystery to him (she kept her seasonings a secret) but it was endearing to him in that way.

She held so much mystery.

As he watched her there, tired and quiet, he realized what was happening. He began to truly appreciate her, all her efforts, every emotion and dream and every word she spoke.

Her mystery, her wonder, her life and everything she could think or touch, had enveloped him. He could not imagine the days that had come before when she was not there, could not imagine each morning waking without her moving upon his heart in some way.

He was in love.

She only swayed a little, subtly shifting her weight from one foot to the next. She was so tired.

He got up from the couch as she reached for her secret seasonings.

"Nope, stay in there. You can't see them." she said playfully.

She's still so funny, even when she's so tired, he thought.

He walked into the kitchen and stood behind her, wrapping his arms around her waist as she spread her secrets on the rice.

One little bit of the secrets that she kept.

He kissed her cheek, and rested his head on her shoulder.

"I love you." he said.

"I love you, too." was her reply.

He hoped it would always be her reply.

The rice was never better than it was that night.

"In the end, I find only you standing by the open door, arms extended, your eyes alight. You beckon me through the door, into the blinding whiteness of eternity, and your arms close around me. Embraced by that freedom, I breathe in you alone. And live eternally. Only you."

Daniel Luke Nunley

Tomorrow is your birthday.

I know I won't be able to see you. It's upsetting, but its life. We both work.

I have something planned for us soon. It's funny, in a way; by the time you read this, it will have come and gone.

It feels a bit odd writing in this tense knowing it will be several weeks before you're able to read it. But there is something stirring around that I can't quite put my finger on. This bears an unburdening.

You told me today what had happened, and I know you must have been upset, frightened. It was upsetting to me, too. I've been praying for everything.

There has been some sort of distance lately I can't quite grasp. I'm wondering if it is just me, or if it was something I said or did. The sort of thinking that drives you crazy, you know?

We're not the best in the world and communicating with each other, but I think it's something we're getting better at. Relationships are work; they're never perfect. The reward is always greater than the effort.

I know sometimes it feels like things are rough, but I want you to know through and through that I'm never going to stop trying, and I'll only ever be honest with you.

I don't want to run everything down, and make everything complicated. It's just simple.

I'll always be there for you.

Always.

i slip out of a sanctuary with tangible bitterness that reverberates from wall to wall, all the falsehoods and the counterfeit values and masquerades of contentedness that i share

i tiptoe out of the door and to my car (parked in the rear) and pull a donation card pilfered from the back of a pew out of my pocket

and scribble a line for you like a store bought poem

i'll give it to you for a cheap smile and a look

and i'll continue to fight my way through all of this with a forgery or a simple word or two

and i will never craft my words beforehand, even if i should

but you

you will look at me as if i plan our dialogue like a charade and call me a charlatan or even say nothing

just fight for words frustrated with the way i articulate or the words that i choose

and try to believe that i mean what i say

and if i can never convince you of my sincerity, and if you fight back the words you want to say to me

i can craft a line for you that will open the skies and give you the stars and the moon and the sun

and all the things you never asked me for

i am no imposter

and don't be afraid to hurt me

I believe someday we will change the world.

I cannot say why or how or when or if it will mean anything to anyone, few or many, but I believe it.

I need to make this clear. There is only one ultimate love, and that is Christ.

I could maybe throw bible verses onto the table and examine this or that, but this is not the time.

I believe that when the time for that comes, we will change this world.

But it's HIS time.

I just feel I'm supposed to put it out there.

God is love, the creator and the spirit and the embodiment. There is no love but Him, including the love he creates, the love he lets us give to each other, the love that he poured out nailed to a tree.

God is love. There is nothing greater.

I know that in the end, I will be dissatisfied with what I've said here.
Upset at the poor quality, the things that I could have clarified, the things I forgot to say.

But there will always be more for me to say to you.

This has been a staggering journey for me, whether you realize it or not. For you to come along and completely shatter all of my pretensions and expectations, I'm astounded.

Thankful.

Frightened.

And blessed.

I expect that when I am able to give this to you, I will be completely embarrassed and upset with it.

But if I can get one smile out of you from it, I'll be happy.

There will always be something else for me to say, something else for me to discover about you, a new way to experience who you are and what you mean to me.

You're a part of me. I hope that's ok.

I hope it will always be that way.

I'm excited and terrified for whatever is going to come our way. In the end, I know it will be ok.

Always.

it's a struggle to find the right words to tell you what all of this is

the way you have been embedded within me like a root, branch to branch and leaf to leaf

deep-seated and connected and feeling by feeling i discover it is incomprehensible the ways that you dig into me and reside, tendril by tendril and breath by breath and hand in hand

existing and dying and being reborn second by second

and the images made in the stars that reflect the journey and the sun and your inflections

beat by beat by beat

the heart of a universe surrounded by a thousand others of infinite sphere and vastness and the ways that our universe is held in the palm of a hand or the pulse of a heart like a new creation so infinitesimal yet of such consequence

and it is you, you and i

take my eyes and hands and feet ears and touch, take my mind and soul and body and all of it

you have my heart, and thus you have it all

and fiber by fiber replace my selfishness and insecurities and replace them with you and dream

beat by beat, hand in hand, step by step

take my universe, and dream

dream with me

"And I look into your eyes for one last time…and I look into
your eyes because you're mine-because you're minc."

Kevin Max

I love you.